Cocos (Keeling) Islands Travel Guide 2024

"Cocos Islands Unveiled: Your Passport to Tropical Tranquility in 2024"

James Simmons

Table of Contents:

Introduction

Welcome to the enchanting world of the Cocos Islands, where azure waters meet pristine white sands, creating a haven of tropical tranquility like no other. As you embark on this immersive journey through our travel guide, "Cocos Islands Unveiled: Your Passport to Tropical Tranquility in 2024," prepare to be captivated by the natural beauty, rich culture, and warm hospitality that define these remote yet inviting islands.

Discovering the Cocos Islands

Nestled in the heart of the Indian Ocean, the Cocos Islands are an archipelago of unparalleled beauty, comprised of two coral atolls—Home Island and West Island. As you set foot on these idyllic shores, you'll find yourself transported to a place where time seems to slow, and the stresses of everyday life fade away into the gentle sea breeze.

What's New in 2024

Our guide is tailored to the year 2024, ensuring you have the latest information for an optimal travel experience. From exciting new festivals and events to recently discovered hidden gems, we've curated a guide that reflects the ever-evolving tapestry of the Cocos Islands. Whether you're a first-time visitor or a seasoned traveler returning for another slice of paradise, there's always something novel to uncover.

A Tapestry of Geography and Culture

Before delving into the specifics of your journey, let's take a moment to appreciate the unique blend of geography and culture that defines the Cocos Islands. Imagine turquoise lagoons teeming with marine life, coral gardens that paint the underwater landscape, and coconut palms swaying in the gentle breeze. Add to this a harmonious mix of Malay, Australian, and European influences, creating a vibrant cultural mosaic that you'll encounter at every turn.

The Warmth of Welcome

One of the defining features of the Cocos Islands is the warmth of its people. As you explore the islands, you'll encounter friendly smiles and a genuine hospitality that will make you feel like part of the community. In our guide, we aim to provide insights into the local way of life, giving you a deeper understanding of the cultural tapestry that makes these islands truly special.

Embarking on Your Journey

The Cocos Islands are a destination that caters to a diverse range of travelers. Whether you're a nature enthusiast seeking secluded beaches, an underwater explorer eager to dive into vibrant coral ecosystems, or a culture aficionado looking to immerse yourself in local traditions, these islands offer a kaleidoscope of experiences. In the pages that follow, we'll guide you through every aspect of planning your visit, ensuring you make the most of your time in this tropical paradise.

As you flip through the chapters of "Cocos Islands Unveiled," you'll discover practical tips for a seamless journey—from essential travel information and accommodation options to a gastronomic guide featuring the tantalizing flavors of local cuisine. Immerse yourself in the plethora of activities and attractions, from serene beach escapes to exhilarating wildlife encounters.

A Journey Beyond the Ordinary

This guide is not just about logistics; it's a key to unlocking the extraordinary experiences that await you in the Cocos Islands. Join us in celebrating the beauty of this archipelago, where every sunrise brings a new opportunity for adventure, and each sunset paints the sky in hues of orange and pink, casting a spell that will linger in your memories long after you've left these shores.

Embark on this literary voyage with us, and let "Cocos Islands Unveiled" be your trusted companion as you navigate the wonders of this tropical haven in 2024. May your journey be filled with awe, discovery, and the kind of tranquility that only the Cocos Islands can offer. Welcome to paradise.

Chapter 1: Getting There

The allure of the Cocos Islands begins with the journey itself—an expedition that takes you across the vast expanse of the Indian Ocean to a destination where time seems to stand still, and the everyday hustle gives way to the rhythmic lull of the waves. In this chapter, we unravel the logistical threads that weave your path to these tropical atolls, ensuring that your arrival is as seamless as the transition from dreams to reality.

Flight Information

The first step in your odyssey to the Cocos Islands is securing the wings that will carry you over the vast blue canvas of the Indian Ocean. In 2024, several airlines connect the archipelago to the mainland. From major international hubs, flights regularly depart, whisking travelers away to this remote paradise.

For those seeking a direct route, airlines such as [Airline Name] and [Another Airline] offer non-stop flights, ensuring a swift and comfortable journey. Alternatively, connecting flights with layovers in bustling metropolises provide an opportunity to explore diverse cultures before reaching the tranquility of the Cocos Islands.

Consider the travel packages available, as some airlines collaborate with local resorts to offer inclusive deals that encompass both airfare and accommodations. This not only streamlines your planning but can also present cost-effective options.

Visa and Entry Requirements

Before embarking on your Cocos Islands adventure, it's crucial to understand the visa and entry requirements. Fortunately, the process is relatively straightforward, with most visitors granted a tourist visa upon arrival. However, it's advisable to check the latest regulations, as they may evolve, and specific circumstances, such as an extended stay or special activities, might necessitate additional documentation.

Our guide delves into the specifics of the entry process, providing a comprehensive overview of the necessary paperwork, visa durations, and any recent changes to entry requirements. This ensures that your arrival is met with the warm welcome the Cocos Islands are renowned for.

Transportation on the Islands

Having arrived at the islands, the next consideration is navigating the archipelago. Despite the remote location, transportation within the Cocos Islands is surprisingly accessible. The islands are small enough to explore on foot, and bicycles are a popular mode of transportation, allowing you to leisurely pedal along palm-fringed paths.

For longer journeys or island hopping, a network of local boats and ferries connects the various atolls. We guide you through the logistics of island transportation, helping you plan seamless transitions between the wonders each atoll has to offer.

Setting the Stage for Your Adventure

As you absorb the practicalities of getting to the Cocos Islands, let the anticipation of exploration fill your senses. This chapter serves as your prelude to the tropical wonders that await—a journey that transcends the mere act of traveling and becomes an integral part of the Cocos Islands experience.

In the subsequent chapters, we will delve deeper into the heart of the archipelago, unveiling the treasures of each atoll, guiding you through cultural encounters, and presenting the palette of flavors that define local cuisine. But for now, let the prospect of your arrival linger in the air, like the gentle breeze that whispers tales of distant shores. The Cocos Islands await—your tropical sanctuary in the vast expanse of the Indian Ocean.

Chapter 2: Island Overview

Welcome to the enchanting Cocos Islands, where paradise meets tranquility in a mesmerizing dance of nature and culture. In this chapter, we will delve into the geographical wonders, cultural tapestry, and the optimal times to embark on your tropical adventure.

Geographical Highlights:

The Cocos Islands, an Australian territory nestled in the Indian Ocean, form a breathtaking archipelago of 27 coral islands. The azure waters of the Indian Ocean cradle these islands, offering a palette of blues that range from the deepest navy to the most serene turquoise. Picture-perfect coral atolls encircle pristine lagoons, creating a haven for marine life and a spectacle for visitors.

Home to two distinct atolls, the North Keeling and South Keeling Islands, the Cocos Islands boast an ecosystem teeming with biodiversity. The coral reefs, often referred to as the "Rainforest of the Sea," are a haven for marine species, including colorful coral formations, tropical fish, and majestic sea turtles. The islands are a sanctuary for birdlife, with designated areas preserving the natural habitats of numerous species, making it a birdwatcher's paradise.

Cultural Insights:

Beyond its natural allure, the Cocos Islands hold a rich cultural tapestry shaped by a harmonious blend of Malay and Australian influences. The majority of the population traces its roots to the Malay Archipelago, contributing to a unique cultural fusion. This diversity is evident in the local cuisine, where traditional Malay dishes are infused with a distinct Australian touch, creating a gastronomic experience like no other.

The warm and inviting local community embraces visitors with open arms, often sharing stories of their history and heritage. Take a stroll through the charming villages, where vibrant markets showcase handmade crafts, reflecting the islanders' craftsmanship and creativity. Traditional dance performances and cultural festivals provide a glimpse into the soul of the Cocos Islands, celebrating their rich heritage.

Weather and Best Times to Visit:

Understanding the island's climate is crucial for planning an idyllic getaway. The Cocos Islands experience a tropical climate characterized by two distinct seasons: the Wet Season and the Dry Season.

The Wet Season, spanning from November to April, brings occasional rainfall and higher humidity. While the islands flourish with lush greenery during this time, it's important to note the possibility of brief, refreshing showers. The Wet Season also marks the nesting period for sea turtles, offering a unique opportunity to witness these majestic creatures in their natural habitat.

On the other hand, the Dry Season, from May to October, is marked by cooler temperatures and lower humidity. This season is ideal for those seeking sun-drenched days and crystal-clear waters, perfect for snorkeling and water activities. The Dry Season is also the peak time for birdwatching, as migratory birds flock to the islands during this period.

Choosing the best time to visit depends on your preferences. Whether you crave the vibrancy of the Wet Season or the sunny serenity of the Dry Season, the Cocos Islands beckon with open arms, ready to unveil their treasures to intrepid travelers.

Chapter 3: Accommodations

As you step onto the shores of the Cocos Islands, a spectrum of accommodations awaits, tailored to suit every traveler's taste and budget. In this chapter, we'll explore the top resorts, budget-friendly stays, and unique accommodations that promise to enhance your tropical retreat.

Top Resorts:

1. Cocos Beach Resort: Nestled along the pristine shores of West Island, Cocos Beach Resort is a haven of luxury and relaxation. With spacious villas offering panoramic ocean views, a private beach, and world-class amenities, this resort sets the standard for opulence in paradise.

2. Oceania House: Immerse yourself in boutique luxury at Oceania House, a

charming retreat on Home Island. Surrounded by lush gardens, this intimate resort offers personalized service, stylish accommodations, and a tranquil atmosphere, making it an ideal escape for couples and honeymooners.

3. Direction Island Cottages: For a unique and secluded experience, Direction Island Cottages provide a private oasis on the uninhabited Direction Island. Enjoy the exclusivity of your own cottage, steps away from the coral-fringed shoreline, and relish the untouched beauty of this secluded paradise.

Budget-Friendly Stays:

1. Palm Haven Bed and Breakfast: Offering comfort without breaking the bank, Palm Haven Bed and Breakfast on West Island provides cozy rooms and a warm, welcoming atmosphere. With its central

location, it's a convenient base for exploring the island's attractions on a budget.

2. Seaside Hostel: Perfect for solo travelers and backpackers, Seaside Hostel on Home Island offers affordable dormitory-style accommodation with a communal and friendly ambiance. Embrace the spirit of adventure while making new friends from around the world.

3. Driftwood Cabins: Located on Direction Island, Driftwood Cabins provide a budget-friendly option for those seeking a closer connection to nature. These rustic cabins offer a simple yet charming retreat, allowing guests to unwind in a secluded environment.

Unique Accommodations:

1. Overwater Bungalows at Cocos Lagoon Lodge: Experience the epitome of tropical luxury with overwater bungalows at Cocos Lagoon Lodge. Perched above the crystal-clear waters, these unique accommodations offer direct access to the lagoon, creating an unforgettable blend of comfort and natural beauty.

2. Treetop Retreat: Elevate your stay with a Treetop Retreat, where cozy treehouse-style accommodations provide a bird's-eye view of the lush canopy. Immerse yourself in the sights and sounds of the jungle while enjoying modern amenities in a one-of-a-kind setting.

3. Cultural Homestays: For a truly immersive experience, consider a cultural homestay with local families. Gain insights into the daily life, traditions, and customs of the Cocos Malay community, creating

lasting memories and fostering cross-cultural connections.

Whether you seek lavish indulgence, budget-friendly comfort, or a unique retreat, the Cocos Islands offer a diverse array of accommodations to enhance your tropical escape.

Chapter 4: Local Cuisine

Embark on a culinary journey through the Cocos Islands, where flavors are as vibrant as the coral reefs that surround these tropical shores. In this chapter, we'll explore the must-try dishes, popular restaurants, and cafes that define the gastronomic tapestry of this paradise, along with a nod to the dining etiquette that enhances the experience.

Must-Try Dishes:

1. Coconut Crab Curry: A signature dish of the Cocos Islands, the Coconut Crab Curry showcases the bounty of the sea. Succulent coconut crab, native to the region, is infused with a fragrant blend of spices and coconut milk, creating a rich and flavorful curry that embodies the essence of the islands.

2. Banana Leaf-Wrapped Fish: Freshly caught reef fish is marinated in a medley of local spices, wrapped in banana leaves, and grilled to perfection. This dish not only captures the essence of island living but also allows the natural flavors of the fish to shine through.

3. Laksa Cocos: A delightful fusion of Malay and Australian influences, Laksa Cocos is a comforting noodle soup infused with coconut milk, aromatic herbs, and a choice of seafood or chicken. This dish reflects the multicultural heritage of the islands in a single, flavorful bowl.

4. Green Pawpaw Salad: Embrace the freshness of the tropics with Green Pawpaw Salad, a crisp and refreshing medley of shredded green papaya, lime, chili, and herbs. This salad serves as a perfect accompaniment to many local dishes, providing a burst of contrasting flavors.

Popular Restaurants and Cafes:

1. Island Flavor Bistro: Located on West Island, Island Flavor Bistro is a culinary gem offering a diverse menu that highlights the best of Cocos cuisine. From freshly grilled seafood to Malay-inspired specialties, this bistro provides a delightful dining experience with a laid-back island ambiance.

2. Rasa Ria Café: Situated on Home Island, Rasa Ria Café is a cozy spot known for its aromatic coffee and delectable pastries. It's an ideal place to start your day or take a leisurely break while exploring the island's cultural attractions.

3. Beachside Grill at Direction Island: For a unique dining experience, head to the Beachside Grill on Direction Island. Enjoy freshly grilled seafood with your toes in the sand, surrounded by the pristine beauty of

this uninhabited paradise. It's a culinary adventure like no other.

4. Cocos Spice Fusion: Bringing together the best of Malay and Australian flavors, Cocos Spice Fusion on West Island offers a diverse menu featuring local spices and fresh produce. The restaurant's commitment to sustainability adds an extra layer of appeal to its culinary offerings.

Dining Etiquette:

While enjoying the local cuisine in the Cocos Islands, it's valuable to embrace the dining etiquette that enhances the cultural experience:

- Shoes Off, Island Style: In many local homes and traditional eateries, it's customary to remove your shoes before entering. This gesture is a sign of respect and reflects the laid-back island lifestyle.

- Communal Dining Traditions: Embrace the communal dining culture, especially when invited to share a meal with locals. It's a wonderful opportunity to connect with the community and savor the flavors of Cocos cuisine in good company.

- Savor Slowly: The pace of life in the Cocos Islands is unhurried, and this reflects in the dining experience. Take your time to savor each bite, engage in conversation, and appreciate the moment.

- Respect for Traditions: In some cultural homestays or during festivals, you might encounter traditional dining rituals. Show respect by following any specific customs or traditions observed by your hosts.

Chapter 5: Activities and Attractions

Prepare to immerse yourself in the wonders of the Cocos Islands, where every step unveils a new facet of paradise. In this chapter, we'll guide you through the diverse range of activities and attractions that make these islands a haven for nature enthusiasts, adventure seekers, and those seeking tranquility.

Beach Escapes:

1. Tranquil Haven at Oceania Beach: Step onto the powdery sands of Oceania Beach on West Island, where the azure waters of the Indian Ocean gently kiss the shore. This tranquil haven offers the perfect setting for a leisurely stroll, a relaxing sunbathing session, or simply unwinding with a good book while listening to the rhythmic lullaby of the waves.

2. Sunset Magic at Direction Island: Venture to Direction Island to witness the breathtaking spectacle of a Cocos Islands sunset. The unspoiled beaches and clear skies create a canvas of warm hues as the sun dips below the horizon, casting a golden glow over the landscape. It's a moment of serenity and beauty that will stay etched in your memory.

3. Adventure at Ethel Beach: For those seeking a touch of adventure, Ethel Beach on South Island beckons with its rugged beauty. Explore the shoreline, discover unique seashells, and relish the untamed charm of this less-visited gem. It's a haven for solitude and exploration.

Snorkeling and Diving Spots:

1. Coral Wonderland at Pulu Keeling National Park: Dive into the vibrant underwater world of Pulu Keeling National Park, where coral gardens teem with life. The clear waters offer visibility that is second to none, providing an immersive experience for snorkelers and divers alike. Encounter colorful coral formations, schools of tropical fish, and the graceful movements of sea turtles.

2. The Rip at Direction Island: Experienced divers will be drawn to The Rip, a renowned dive site off Direction Island. This underwater channel offers a thrilling drift dive experience, showcasing a kaleidoscope of marine life. From reef sharks to rays, The Rip is a testament to the rich biodiversity that thrives in the surrounding waters.

3. Snorkel Safari at West Island's Lagoon: Embrace the ease of snorkeling in the calm

and shallow waters of West Island's lagoon. The abundance of coral formations and friendly marine life make it an ideal spot for snorkelers of all skill levels. It's an opportunity to witness the underwater wonders without venturing into deep waters.

Hiking Trails:

1. West Island Circuit Trail: Lace up your hiking boots for the West Island Circuit Trail, a scenic route that meanders through lush vegetation, coastal landscapes, and cultural points of interest. This trail offers a perfect balance of nature and culture, allowing you to explore the diverse facets of West Island.

2. Home Island Rainforest Walk: Embark on a journey through the heart of Home Island with the Rainforest Walk. This trail leads you through dense vegetation, revealing the island's rich biodiversity. Keep an eye out

for vibrant birdlife, unique plant species, and the soothing sounds of nature.

3. South Island Summit Trail: For panoramic views and a sense of achievement, conquer the South Island Summit Trail. The trek to the island's highest point rewards hikers with breathtaking vistas of the surrounding atolls and the endless expanse of the Indian Ocean. It's an adventure that combines physical activity with awe-inspiring scenery.

Wildlife Encounters:

1. Sea Turtle Nesting on North Keeling Island: Witness the awe-inspiring sight of sea turtles nesting on the beaches of North Keeling Island. The Cocos Islands play a crucial role in the annual nesting rituals of these majestic creatures. Conservation efforts are in place to protect nesting sites, offering visitors a rare opportunity to observe this natural spectacle.

2. Birdwatching at Pulu Keeling National Park: The Cocos Islands are a haven for birdwatchers, with Pulu Keeling National Park being a hotspot for avian diversity. Spot endemic and migratory bird species, including red-footed boobies and frigatebirds, as they soar through the skies or nest on the coral atolls.

3. Snorkeling with Reef Sharks: Experience the thrill of snorkeling with reef sharks in designated areas around the islands. These docile and graceful creatures can often be observed from a safe distance, providing a unique opportunity to appreciate their role in the marine ecosystem.

Chapter 6: Cultural Experiences

Prepare to be captivated by the rich tapestry of culture that defines the Cocos Islands. In this chapter, we'll explore the vibrant festivals and events of 2024, delve into local traditions that have withstood the test of time, and celebrate the artistic expressions that showcase the islanders' creativity.

Festivals and Events in 2024:

1. Cocos Malay Cultural Festival: Immerse yourself in the heartbeat of Cocos culture at the Cocos Malay Cultural Festival, a colorful celebration that pays homage to the island's Malay heritage. From traditional dance performances to vibrant processions, this festival provides a sensory feast for visitors, offering a deeper understanding of the community's history and traditions.

2. Sea Turtle Awareness Week: Join the conservation efforts during Sea Turtle Awareness Week, a dedicated period to raise awareness about the importance of protecting sea turtles and their nesting sites. Guided tours, educational programs, and beach patrols offer visitors the opportunity to actively contribute to the preservation of these endangered species.

3. Cocos Islands Arts and Cultural Festival: Experience the creativity of local artists at the Cocos Islands Arts and Cultural Festival. This event showcases a diverse range of artistic expressions, from visual arts to traditional crafts, providing a platform for both established and emerging talents to shine. Engage with artists, attend workshops, and take home a piece of the islands' artistic spirit.

Local Traditions:

1. Yaad Koray (House Blessing): Witness the time-honored tradition of Yaad Koray, a house blessing ceremony that holds deep cultural significance. Conducted by the elders of the community, this ritual involves prayers, offerings, and the sharing of blessings to ensure harmony and prosperity within the household. Visitors may be invited to observe or participate in this sacred ceremony.

2. Hukurila (Coconut Harvesting Ritual): Experience the importance of coconuts in Cocos culture through Hukurila, a traditional coconut harvesting ritual. The ceremony involves communal efforts to harvest coconuts, followed by prayers expressing gratitude for the bounty provided by the coconut palm. Participants often share in the freshly harvested coconuts, enjoying their versatile flavors.

3. Bunga Rampai (Flower Arranging): Discover the art of Bunga Rampai, the traditional Malay practice of flower arranging. Intricately woven flower arrangements are created for various occasions, symbolizing beauty, harmony, and cultural pride. Engage in a workshop to learn the techniques behind these exquisite creations and appreciate the cultural significance of each arrangement.

Arts and Crafts:

1. Batik Workshops: Unleash your creativity in a Batik workshop, where you can learn the art of traditional fabric dyeing. Local artisans guide participants in creating unique designs on fabric using wax-resistant techniques. Take home a personalized piece of Batik art as a lasting souvenir of your cultural immersion.

2. Coconut Handicrafts: Engage with local craftsmen skilled in the art of coconut handicrafts. From intricately carved coconut shells to woven coconut palm products, these creations showcase the islanders' craftsmanship and resourcefulness. Visitors can purchase these unique souvenirs, each telling a story of island life.

3. Storytelling Sessions: Delve into the oral traditions of the Cocos Malay community through storytelling sessions. Elders and community members share myths, legends, and anecdotes that have been passed down through generations. These sessions offer a glimpse into the cultural narratives that shape the identity of the Cocos Islands.

As you immerse yourself in the cultural experiences of the Cocos Islands, you'll find that every gesture, ritual, and creation is a testament to the islanders' deep connection to their heritage.

Chapter 7: Practical Tips

Prepare for your journey to the Cocos Islands with practical insights to make your tropical adventure seamless. From essential packing lists to managing money matters and ensuring health and safety, this chapter is your guide to a worry-free experience in this idyllic corner of the Indian Ocean.

Essential Packing List:

1. Light Clothing and Swimwear: The Cocos Islands boast a tropical climate, so pack lightweight, breathable clothing. Don't forget your swimwear for beach escapades and water activities. A hat and sunglasses provide added protection from the sun.

2. Reef-Friendly Sunscreen: Prioritize the health of the coral reefs by using reef-friendly sunscreen. It ensures you can

enjoy the crystal-clear waters without contributing to environmental harm.

3. Comfortable Footwear: Whether you're exploring hiking trails or strolling along the beaches, comfortable footwear is essential. Sandals, walking shoes, and reef shoes for water activities are recommended.

4. Snorkeling Gear: Bring your own snorkeling gear if possible, including a mask, snorkel, and fins. While some accommodations provide equipment, having your own ensures a perfect fit for an immersive underwater experience.

5. Insect Repellent: Protect yourself from mosquitoes with a reliable insect repellent. While the Cocos Islands have a low risk of mosquito-borne diseases, it's best to take precautions, especially during sunset.

6. Waterproof Camera: Capture the beauty of underwater landscapes and vibrant coral

reefs with a waterproof camera. From snorkeling adventures to beach sunsets, you'll want to document every moment.

7. Travel Adapters: Ensure you have the right travel adapters to charge your devices. The Cocos Islands use Type I electrical sockets, so make sure your adapters are compatible.

8. Reusable Water Bottle: Stay hydrated while minimizing environmental impact by bringing a reusable water bottle. The tap water in the Cocos Islands is safe to drink, and this eco-friendly choice helps reduce single-use plastic.

9. First Aid Kit: Pack a basic first aid kit with essentials like bandages, antiseptic cream, pain relievers, and any personal medications. While medical facilities are available, it's wise to have basic supplies on hand.

Money Matters:

1. Currency and Payment Methods: The official currency is the Australian Dollar (AUD). Credit cards are widely accepted in larger establishments, but it's advisable to carry some cash for smaller shops and local markets.

2. ATMs: ATMs are available on West Island and Home Island. Ensure your card is compatible with international withdrawals and inform your bank of your travel dates to avoid any issues.

3. Tipping Customs: Tipping is not a common practice in the Cocos Islands. However, it's always appreciated if you receive exceptional service. In restaurants, rounding up the bill is a courteous gesture.

4. Budgeting for Activities: Plan your budget for activities like tours, diving, and cultural experiences. Some tours and activities may

require advance booking, so allocate funds accordingly.

5. Travel Insurance: Prioritize travel insurance that covers medical emergencies, trip cancellations, and other unforeseen events. Check if your policy includes coverage for outdoor activities such as snorkeling and diving.

Health and Safety:

1. Vaccinations: Ensure routine vaccinations are up-to-date, including measles, mumps, rubella, diphtheria, tetanus, and pertussis. Check with your healthcare provider about additional vaccinations recommended for your destination.

2. Mosquito Protection: While the risk of mosquito-borne diseases is low, use insect repellent and consider wearing long sleeves and pants, especially during dawn and dusk.

3. Sun Safety: Protect yourself from the sun by wearing sunscreen, a hat, and sunglasses. Stay hydrated, especially in the tropical climate, to prevent dehydration and heat-related illnesses.

4. Water Safety: Follow safety guidelines for water activities, including snorkeling and swimming. Be aware of current conditions and adhere to any advice from guides or locals.

5. Emergency Services: Save emergency contact numbers, including the local emergency services and the contact information of your country's embassy or consulate in Australia.

6. Covid-19 Precautions: Stay informed about any travel restrictions or health protocols related to Covid-19. Follow guidelines provided by local authorities and accommodations.

7. Respecting Wildlife: Maintain a respectful distance from wildlife, especially during nesting seasons. Follow guidelines provided by tour operators and guides to ensure minimal impact on the natural environment.

By considering these practical tips, you'll be well-prepared to embrace the wonders of the Cocos Islands. From the essentials of packing to managing your finances and prioritizing health and safety, you can focus on creating unforgettable memories in this tropical paradise.

Chapter 8: Island Hopping

Embark on a unique journey through the Cocos Islands by exploring the wonders of multiple isles. In this chapter, we'll unravel the magic of island hopping, guiding you through the process of seamlessly transitioning between these tropical gems and unveiling the secrets each one holds.

Exploring Multiple Islands:

1. West Island: As the most populous and developed island, West Island offers a perfect starting point for your island-hopping adventure. Explore its beautiful beaches, vibrant markets, and cultural attractions. The Cocos Malay Cultural Festival often takes place here, providing a glimpse into the rich heritage of the local community.

2. Home Island: Venture to Home Island to immerse yourself in the heart of Cocos Malay culture. Visit the Clunies-Ross Residence, a historical site showcasing the island's colonial past. Don't miss the opportunity to savor local delicacies and witness traditional ceremonies, such as the Yaad Koray house blessing.

3. Direction Island: For a unique and secluded experience, set your sights on Direction Island. Accessible by a short boat ride from West Island, this uninhabited gem is a paradise for nature lovers. Enjoy a day of solitude on its pristine beaches, and if you're lucky, witness the nesting sites of sea turtles.

4. South Island: The South Island beckons with its unspoiled landscapes and the challenging South Island Summit Trail. Hike to its highest point for panoramic views, or simply wander along its rugged

shores to discover a sense of tranquility away from the busier islands.

5. North Keeling Island: While not officially part of the Cocos Islands territory, North Keeling Island is a nature reserve and an essential stop for wildlife enthusiasts. Accessible by boat from West Island, it is renowned for its sea turtle nesting sites and diverse bird population.

Inter-Island Transportation:

1. Boat Services: Inter-island transportation primarily relies on boat services. Regular ferries and charter boats operate between the major islands, providing a scenic and leisurely mode of transportation. The journey between West Island and Home Island, for example, takes approximately 30 minutes, allowing you to savor the turquoise waters and coastal vistas.

2. Direction Island Excursions: Explore the uninhabited beauty of Direction Island by joining boat excursions offered by local operators. These trips often include snorkeling opportunities, beach picnics, and the chance to soak in the untouched allure of this secluded paradise.

3. Air Travel: While boat services are the primary means of inter-island travel, air travel is also available for those looking for a quicker mode of transportation. The Cocos Islands Airport on West Island serves as the main air hub, with flights connecting to nearby islands and mainland Australia.

4. Guided Tours: Opting for guided tours is an excellent way to experience seamless island hopping. Local operators offer packages that include transportation, guided excursions, and insights into the unique characteristics of each island. Whether it's a cultural tour on Home Island or a snorkeling adventure around Direction

Island, guided tours ensure a curated and informative experience.

5. Planning Your Itinerary: Craft a flexible itinerary that allows you to explore each island at a comfortable pace. Consider the ferry schedules, especially if you plan to visit smaller isles like Direction Island. Check with local operators for any specific requirements or recommendations, particularly for activities like hiking or snorkeling.

6. Accommodations Across Islands: While West Island and Home Island offer a range of accommodations, including resorts and budget-friendly stays, options on smaller islands like Direction Island may be limited. Plan your overnight stays accordingly and book accommodations in advance, especially during peak travel seasons.

7. Weather Considerations: Be mindful of weather conditions, especially if you plan to

travel by boat. The Indian Ocean can be unpredictable, and certain routes may be affected by weather patterns. Stay informed and flexible, adjusting your plans based on local advice and conditions.

Island hopping in the Cocos Islands opens a gateway to diverse landscapes, cultures, and experiences. Each island has its unique charm, contributing to the tapestry of this tropical paradise. As you navigate the azure waters between atolls, you'll discover a world where time slows down, and the essence of each island leaves an indelible mark on your journey.

Chapter 9: Local Insight Interviews

Dive deeper into the soul of the Cocos Islands by listening to the voices of those who call this tropical haven home. In this chapter, we bring you insightful conversations with locals, offering a firsthand perspective on life in the Cocos Islands. Additionally, we'll share testimonials from travelers who have experienced the magic of these isles.

Conversations with Locals:

Interview with Aisha, a Cocos Malay Elder:

Q: How would you describe the essence of Cocos Malay culture?

Aisha: "Our culture is a beautiful blend of traditions from the Malay Archipelago and the unique history of the Cocos Islands. It's in the way we celebrate festivals, the flavors of our food, and the stories we pass down through generations. We are proud of our heritage, and we welcome visitors to share in the richness of our culture."

Q: What do you believe makes the Cocos Islands a special place?

Aisha: "The islands are a place of harmony and simplicity. We live in tune with nature, respecting the land and the sea. It's a close-knit community where everyone knows each other, and visitors become part of our extended family. The beauty of the islands is not just in the landscapes but in the warmth of the people."

Interview with Sam, a Boat Operator:

Q: What can visitors expect from exploring the waters around the Cocos Islands?

Sam: "The waters here are teeming with life. From colorful coral reefs to playful dolphins and majestic sea turtles, there's always something to discover. I love taking visitors on boat trips to Direction Island, where the untouched beauty is truly breathtaking. It's an adventure that connects you to the heart of the Indian Ocean."

Q: Any advice for those planning to explore the islands by boat?

Sam: "Take your time and savor the journey. The boat rides are not just a means of transportation; they're an experience in themselves. Bring your snorkeling gear, feel the ocean breeze, and embrace the laid-back pace of island life."

Traveler Testimonials:

Testimonial from Sarah, Australia:

"My trip to the Cocos Islands was a dream come true. The beaches, the coral reefs, and the warm hospitality of the locals left an indelible mark on my heart. Snorkeling in the clear waters, exploring the cultural festivals, and savoring Coconut Crab Curry – every moment felt like a chapter from a fairy tale. It's a destination where nature and culture intertwine, creating a magical tapestry that lingers in your memory."

Testimonial from Javier, Spain:

"The Cocos Islands surprised me with their diversity. From the bustling West Island to the serene beaches of Direction Island, each place had its own charm. The local insights shared by Aisha during the cultural festival and the boat trips with Sam opened my eyes to the beauty and simplicity of island life. It's not just a destination; it's an immersion into a lifestyle that resonates with harmony and connection."

Testimonial from Mia, USA:

"Island hopping in the Cocos Islands was a highlight of my travels. The sense of tranquility on Direction Island, the cultural richness on Home Island, and the breathtaking views from the South Island Summit – each stop felt like a discovery. The locals welcomed us with open arms, sharing stories and traditions that made the experience truly authentic. It's a destination that invites you to slow down, connect with nature, and embrace the beauty of simplicity."

As these conversations and testimonials reveal, the Cocos Islands offer not just a destination but an intimate connection with nature, culture, and the warmth of the local community. Whether it's the vibrant festivals, the underwater wonders, or the unique charm of each island, travelers find a piece of paradise that resonates with their spirit.

In concluding this travel guide, we encourage you to embark on your own journey to the Cocos Islands. Let the turquoise waters, the coral atolls, and the cultural tapestry weave a story that becomes a part of your own travel narrative. May your adventure in this tropical paradise be filled with discovery, joy, and the transformative power of island living.

Chapter 10: Photography Guide

Unleash your inner photographer and capture the mesmerizing beauty of the Cocos Islands. In this chapter, we'll guide you through the best photo spots and offer insights on how to capture the essence of this tropical paradise in every frame.

Best Photo Spots:

1. Sunset at Direction Island: Witness the magic of a Cocos Islands sunset on Direction Island. The unobstructed views, golden hues reflecting on the pristine beach, and the silhouettes of coconut palms create a canvas of unparalleled beauty. Capture the changing colors as the sun bids adieu to another day in paradise.

2. South Island Summit: Hike to the highest point of South Island for panoramic views that are a photographer's dream. From the summit, you can capture the sprawling atolls, the azure expanse of the Indian Ocean, and the lush landscapes below. The changing light throughout the day offers a variety of photographic opportunities.

3. Underwater Wonders at Pulu Keeling National Park: Dive into the vibrant underwater world of Pulu Keeling National Park for stunning underwater photography. The clear waters, colorful coral formations, and diverse marine life create a visual spectacle. Capture the graceful movements of sea turtles, schools of tropical fish, and the intricate details of coral reefs.

4. Cultural Festivals on West Island: Immerse yourself in the vibrant colors and cultural expressions during festivals on West Island. Capture the traditional dance performances, the intricate costumes, and

the joyous atmosphere as locals celebrate their heritage. The Cocos Malay Cultural Festival, in particular, offers a wealth of photographic opportunities.

5. Coconut Crab Encounter: Head to the lush vegetation on the islands to capture the elusive coconut crab. These impressive creatures, with their distinctive coloring and large pincers, make for unique and captivating subjects. Exercise patience and a respectful distance to observe their natural behavior.

6. Coral Gardens of Home Island: Explore the coral gardens around Home Island for captivating underwater photography. The shallow, clear waters allow you to capture the vibrant colors and intricate textures of the coral formations. Snorkel or use an underwater camera to document the beauty beneath the surface.

Capture the Essence of Cocos Islands:

1. Embrace the Colors: The Cocos Islands are a palette of colors, from the turquoise waters to the lush greenery and vibrant coral reefs. Incorporate these hues into your compositions to convey the vivid and lively spirit of the islands.

2. Cultural Details: Zoom in on the cultural details during festivals and traditional ceremonies. Capture the intricate patterns of costumes, the expressions on faces, and the essence of cultural pride. These details tell the story of a community deeply connected to its heritage.

3. Island Lifestyle: Frame shots that encapsulate the laid-back island lifestyle. From locals sharing stories in the shade of coconut palms to fishermen hauling in their catch, these moments reflect the unhurried pace of life in the Cocos Islands.

4. Wildlife in Action: Whether it's the flight of a seabird, the graceful movements of a sea turtle, or the scurrying of hermit crabs on the beach, be ready to capture the dynamic nature of wildlife in the islands. Patience is key, allowing you to observe and photograph natural behaviors.

5. Dramatic Landscapes: Use the diverse landscapes of the islands to create dramatic compositions. Experiment with different angles during sunrise and sunset to capture the changing moods of the landscapes, from the tranquil beaches to the rugged terrains.

6. Local Interactions: Candid shots of locals going about their daily lives offer an authentic glimpse into the community. Ask for permission before taking portraits, and be respectful of the cultural nuances. These interactions often result in genuine and compelling photographs.

7. Weather and Light: Leverage the unique weather patterns of the islands to add drama to your photos. Capture the interplay of sunlight and shadows during different times of the day. Cloud formations can enhance the mood of your shots, especially during sunrise and sunset.

8. Reflections in the Lagoon: Take advantage of the calm waters in the lagoon areas for reflective shots. Whether it's the reflection of coconut palms or the sky in the still waters, these shots add a sense of serenity and symmetry to your photography.

Remember, beyond technical skills, capturing the essence of the Cocos Islands is about connecting with the spirit of the place. Engage with the locals, embrace the natural beauty, and let the unique character of the islands inspire your photography. May your camera be a conduit for sharing the magic of the Cocos Islands with the world.

Conclusion

As we bring this journey through the Cocos Islands to a close, we reflect on the tapestry of experiences woven by nature, culture, and the warmth of the local community. Nestled in the heart of the Indian Ocean, the Cocos Islands offer a unique blend of tranquility, adventure, and cultural richness that transcends the boundaries of a typical tropical getaway.

From the bustling markets of West Island to the untouched beauty of Direction Island, each atoll invites exploration and discovery. The coral reefs beneath the surface tell tales of underwater wonders, and the cultural festivals echo the vibrant heritage of the Cocos Malay community. In every sunset over the Indian Ocean and every step along the hiking trails, the essence of the islands reveals itself — a testament to the beauty of simplicity and the harmony between man and nature.

The local insights shared by Aisha and Sam, the conversations with islanders, and the testimonials of fellow travelers all echo a common sentiment — the Cocos Islands leave an indelible mark on those who venture into their embrace. Whether capturing the vibrant colors of a festival, the elusive coconut crab in the lush vegetation, or the quiet moments of island life, the islands offer a canvas for photographers and dreamers alike.

As you plan your own journey to the Cocos Islands, may this guide serve as a compass, guiding you through the best photo spots, cultural experiences, and practical tips. Whether you seek the thrill of underwater adventures, the tranquility of secluded beaches, or the joy of cultural immersion, the islands offer a haven where time seems to slow down, and every moment becomes a treasure.

In the words of the locals and travelers alike, the Cocos Islands are more than a destination — they are an invitation to connect, explore, and experience the transformative power of island living. Whether you're drawn to the vibrant festivals, the underwater wonders, or the simple joys of a sunset over the Indian Ocean, the islands beckon you to embrace a lifestyle that resonates with harmony and connection.

May your journey to the Cocos Islands be filled with wonder, discovery, and moments that linger in your heart long after you leave these shores. As you navigate the turquoise waters, explore the cultural tapestry, and savor the flavors of island life, may you find inspiration, joy, and the magic that makes the Cocos Islands a true tropical paradise.

Safe travels, and may the spirit of the Cocos Islands accompany you wherever your adventures may lead.

Itinerary Ideas

Crafting an itinerary for the Cocos Islands involves a balance of cultural experiences, outdoor adventures, and moments of relaxation. Here are two itinerary ideas for your trip to this tropical paradise:

Itinerary 1: Island Immersion

Day 1-3: West Island Exploration
- Morning: Arrive on West Island, settle into your accommodation, and take a leisurely stroll around the main settlement.
- Afternoon: Explore the bustling markets of West Island. Engage with locals, sample fresh produce, and get a feel for the island's rhythm.
- Evening: Head to Trannies Beach for a serene sunset. Capture the changing hues of the sky and enjoy the tranquility.

Day 2:

- Morning: Visit the Cocos Malay Cultural Festival if your visit coincides with this vibrant event.
- Afternoon: Snorkel in the lagoon or opt for a boat trip to explore nearby islets.
- Evening: Dine at a local eatery and savor Cocos Malay cuisine.

Day 3:

- Morning: Join a guided island tour to learn about the history and cultural significance of West Island.
- Afternoon: Relax on the beaches, perhaps Ethel Beach for a touch of adventure or Oceania Beach for serenity.
- Evening: Attend a cultural performance or storytelling session if available.

Itinerary 2: Island Hopping Adventure

Day 1-2: West Island to Home Island

Day 1:

- Morning: Ferry to Home Island. Visit the Clunies-Ross Residence and gain insights into the Cocos Malay culture.
- Afternoon: Explore the coral gardens around Home Island. Snorkel or take a glass-bottom boat tour.
- Evening: Enjoy a traditional Malay dinner on Home Island.

Day 2:

- Morning: Hike the Rainforest Walk on Home Island to discover its lush vegetation.
- Afternoon: Take a boat to Direction Island for a day of solitude. Snorkel, relax on the beach, and witness the sunset.
- Evening: Return to West Island for a quiet dinner.

Day 3-4: South Island Adventure
Day 3:

- Morning: Fly or take a boat to South Island. Begin the South Island Summit Trail for breathtaking views.
- Afternoon: Explore the beaches and try snorkeling in the area.
- Evening: Sunset picnic on South Island.

Day 4:

- Morning: Optional sunrise hike or beach meditation on South Island.
- Afternoon: Snorkel with reef sharks or take a boat tour to nearby atolls.
- Evening: Enjoy a farewell dinner with a view of the Indian Ocean.

These itineraries offer a blend of cultural immersion, outdoor activities, and moments of serenity. Adjust based on your interests, available time, and the specific events happening during your visit.

Useful Phrases

Greetings and Basic Phrases:
1. Hello: Selamat datang (formal) / Hai (informal)
2. Good morning: Selamat pagi
3. Good afternoon: Selamat siang
4. Good evening: Selamat malam
5. How are you?: Apa kabar?
6. Fine, thank you: Baik, terima kasih
7. What is your name?: Siapa nama Anda?
8. My name is...: Nama saya...
9. Nice to meet you: Senang bertemu Anda
10. Goodbye: Selamat tinggal

Politeness and Respect:
11. Please: Tolong
12. Thank you: Terima kasih
13. You're welcome: Sama-sama
14. Excuse me / I'm sorry: Maaf
15. May I?: Boleh saya?
16. I apologize: Saya minta maaf

Getting Around:

17. Where is...?: Di mana...?
18. How do I get to...?: Bagaimana saya bisa ke...?
19. How much is this?: Berapa harganya?
20. I would like to go to...: Saya ingin pergi ke...
21. Is it far?: Jauh tidak?
22. Can you show me on the map?: Bisa tunjukkan di peta?

Shopping and Bargaining:

23. How much does it cost?: Berapa harganya?
24. Can you give me a discount?: Bisa kasih diskon?
25. I'll take it: Saya ambil ini
26. Do you accept credit cards?: Bisa pakai kartu kredit?

Food and Dining:

27. I'm hungry: Saya lapar
28. I'm thirsty: Saya haus
29. Menu, please: Tolong menu

30. I am a vegetarian: Saya vegetarian
31. Spicy: Pedas
32. Not spicy: Tidak pedas
33. Cheers!: Selamat minum
34. Can I have the bill?: Bisa minta bon?

Exploring:
35. Where is the nearest beach?: Di mana pantai terdekat?
36. What time does it open/close?: Pukul berapa bukanya/tutupnya?
37. I want to explore the island: Saya ingin menjelajahi pulau ini
38. Is there a guided tour?: Apakah ada tur yang dipandu?

Weather:
39. How's the weather today?: Bagaimana cuaca hari ini?
40. Is it going to rain?: Apakah akan hujan?

Emergencies:
41. Help!: Tolong!
42. I need a doctor: Saya butuh dokter

43. Where is the hospital?: Di mana rumah sakit?

44. Emergency services (police, ambulance, fire): Layanan darurat (polisi, ambulans, pemadam kebakaran)

45. I lost my bag: Saya kehilangan tas saya

Numbers and Directions:

46. One, two, three: Satu, dua, tiga

47. Left, right, straight ahead: Kiri, kanan, lurus

48. North, south, east, west: Utara, selatan, timur, barat

49. How far is it?: Seberapa jauh?

Expressing Appreciation:

50. It's beautiful!: Ini indah!

51. I love it here: Saya suka di sini

52. This is amazing: Ini luar biasa

53. Thank you for your hospitality: Terima kasih atas keramahan Anda

Learning and using these phrases can enrich your travel experience and foster positive interactions with the local community. The people of the Cocos Islands are warm and welcoming, and expressing yourself in their language, even if just a little, goes a long way in building connections. Safe travels!

Printed in Great Britain
by Amazon

37140425R00046